praise

"A rich collection of poems that take the reader on a deep tour of the psyche. Charting and moving across politics of language, Bell explores love, pain, failure and redemption from a variety of angles. Most of the poems sit at the fragile threshold of instinct and meaning, using symbol and sensation to get to the shock of denouement. This is a significant collection that bears multiple readings, each time yielding something fresh."
MAGDALENA BALL, AUTHOR OF *BLACK COW*

"*Fabric* is spun with threads of imagination, realism, and unanswered questions. Jessica Bell weaves from the outer edges of the human condition to the inner tapestry of the mind, sewing through love, trust, and betrayal. Bell is adept with words and imagery; her edgy tone, both daring and tender, seamlessly captures the hearts and minds of everyday people."
ANGELA FELSTED, AUTHOR OF *CLEAVE*

"Mixing both light and dark subjects, *Fabric* slips as smoothly as silk across the poetry-lover's mind. Bell knows what she's doing, and she won't disappoint with this elegantly textured collection. Truly a treasure!"
MICHELLE DAVIDSON ARGYLE, AUTHOR OF *TRUE COLORS*

"With a deft touch and an acute eye, Jessica Bell weaves humanity into startling vistas, blending the vivid threads of contemporary introspection among a tapestry of tangible scenery. The seamless entwining of the historical with the present, results in a garment the reader may slip on with pleasure, at any moment, and find themselves lost in its intricacies, and more beautiful for its embrace."
VICKY ELLIS, AUTHOR AND POET

about the author

Jessica Bell is an Australian award-winning author and poet, writing and publishing coach, and graphic designer who lives in Athens, Greece. In addition to her novels and poetry collections, and her best-selling *Writing in a Nutshell* series, she has published a variety of works online and in literary journals, including *Writer's Digest*.

Jessica is also the Co-Founder and Publisher of *Vine Leaves Press & Literary Journal*, a singer/songwriter/guitarist, a voice-over actor, and a freelance editor and writer for English Language Teaching publishers world-wide such as Macmillan Education and Education First.

Before she started writing she was just a young woman with a "useless" Bachelor of Arts degree and a waitressing job.

Visit Jessica's website: *jessicabellauthor.com*

Vine Leaves Press
Melbourne, Victoria, Australia

Second Edition
ISBN-13: 978-1-925417-41-8

First edition published by Vine Leaves Press Canada, 2012

This is a work of fiction. Any similarity between the characters and situations within its pages and places or persons, living or dead, is unintentional and co-incidental.

Cover design by Jessica Bell
Interior design by Amie McCracken

National Library of Australia Cataloguing-in-Publication entry (paperback)
Creator: Bell, Jessica Carmen, author.
Title: Fabric / Jessica Bell.
Edition: 2nd edition.
ISBN: 9781925417418 (paperback)
Subjects: Australian poetry.
Dewey Number: A821.4

fabric

jessica bell

Vine Leaves Press
Melbourne, Vic, Australia

"When we constantly ask for miracles, we're unraveling the fabric of the world. A world of continuous miracles would not be a world, it would be a cartoon."
Doug Coupland

contents

εγώ

summer leaves
float in muddy
dry confessions voices

a drink of breath
a shawl to dance
in my own touch

below the soil
the weavers live
they blend me in

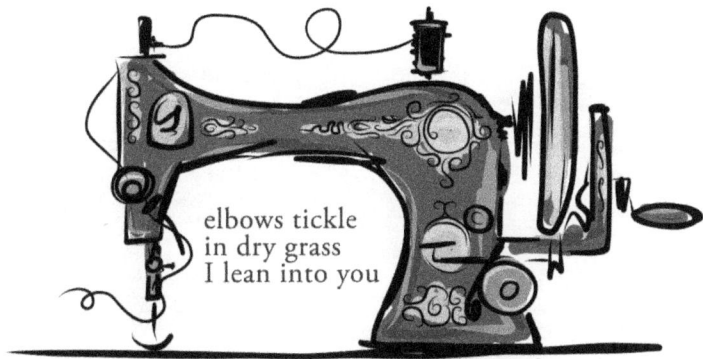

elbows tickle
in dry grass
I lean into you

wrinkles print
waves into my soul
ocean memories

quicksand fills
my thimble with
a clone of earth

no butterfly kisses
ugly flashes
seed through

canvas

Feelings can be broken
when layered paint cracks—

white noise calcified to the tune
of poise and pleasure—Socialism

perched on a paint brush;
an election on canvas.

I snack on written woes;
electronic black mail slips

through automated slots—a grant
to an artist who sells reclusivism

to hermits in dusty boxes.
I cut one open at breakfast,

patterns of hope discoloured
with yoke. And tears.

I purchased my own work.
Hung it on my wall.

Sometimes I like to touch it
with my eyes closed.

breaking the curse

My words create shawls—
they cloak the crazies
on empty nights

like this.

So I pick up a pencil
and press it to my palm—
rendering my thoughts clichéd.
But being welcomed back
will never really be clichéd
as long my return to the village
is kept to

myself.

I sense the weight now
of Euterpe
gnidnib ym no gnitirw;
pins and needles at a party
unwrapping my fingertips
like a Kolossus.

I suppose this would be
a nice place to

Stop.

But the six-month-old curse
needs pushing from my pitiless tongue.

I'll spit air into streaks of lead.

mama's confession

My nails aren't strong enough
to scratch you anymore,
Antoni mou.

I suppose you're relieved.

The old maid's weapons
are blunt; brittle—painted
with layers and layers of pearl
varnish, disguising
the fungus
I've spent years
trying to remove;
to hide from patrons'
judgmental view.

Remember
when you said it grew
to match your blood stains?
You believed every time
I ripped your shirts,
the infection would reappear.
It was punishment
for not feeling, I guess.

I don't watch the news
anymore. But I'd like you
to know, I will write
until you've lived
your thirteen lives.

I hope prison
treats you better
than I did.

flesh

I drop my wedding ring
in holy water.
I hope it repels;
the years
of hate
and hope,
so I can finally relate
to the son we made.

leather

I am today's personality;
an accent of death for those
still trying to live.
I'm scattered through
3D streets
where stray cats
call my name
unaware
that I now live
like a fox skin tent:
psychological warmth
without fur.
I still bleed
where crucified
with practicalities.
I am not a mythical serpent.
I am what vegans
pretend do not exist.

moNemvasia

White-capped tears
no longer soothe
the clefts and valleys
of my cracked skin.
Instead they sting
like pins and burn
away bruised years.

They all see my cliff
faces steep. But I feel
them flat and steady,
where donkey's legs
don't slip nor buckle,
despite my stone being
worn to its satin bone.

Drifting soles shuffle
through hushed alleys
—roads with no ends
or beginnings. But in
the center, the locals
wait. I smell their lust
—ashes in my soul.

the only one left standing

I'm weighed down by a thick need
tangled between a man who doesn't care
a waitress who seems to care
and a conscience that cares too much.

Cuban tunes lace Mexican dreams;
cloud the reality I left behind
tucked under a cushion
on our dirty cream suede couch.

I sip my margarita, watch them dance
feel the thump, the twang, taste the tang.
Señoritas twirl, orange skirts become a blur
behind the mumble and slur of his speech.

Then I remember.
I'm still in Greece.
In the restaurant near the bus stop.
The only one left standing.

εσύ

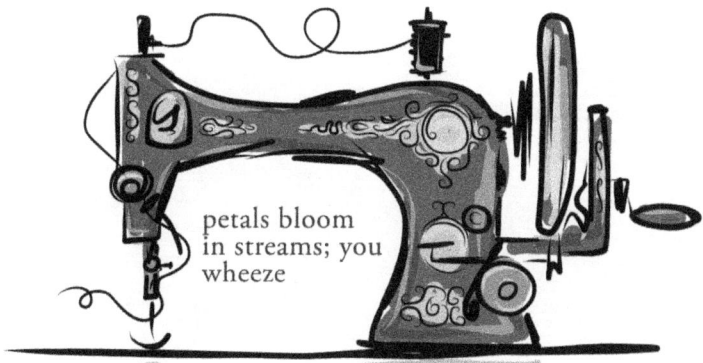

baby basics
cloud your judgement:
akiss her forehead

you peer into
the waters and see
fear reflections

primrose promises
child, you bear angst
in fragrant dinners

petals bloom
in streams; you
wheeze

the soft touches
of cherry powder
colours in your ache

warm breasts leak
nurturing thought—
love stains you

relaxes, five enough
your peep arch
months, not

sugar

You were *Yiayia*.
But I called you *Zacharati*.
That was your name.
It meant *sugar*.

Your parents must have known
that when you aged,
you'd litter your kitchen
bench with it,
when you'd make *halva*,
and wipe your hands
on your fraying apron
exactly seven times a day.

I'd count.
You'd giggle.
Papou would cross himself.

Every day I'd watch
you press baked almonds
into the squishy centers
of the diamond-shaped
brown sweets.

You were granting them hearts.

And that's when you'd bring out the sugar.
And a sieve.

And sprinkle your name all over my world.

scarf

Muzzled by split expectation; lips tacked
with brittle burgundy thread. You open
your mouth to utter censure, teeth bared
behind a web of folk tapestry: ziggy-zaggy
voices, sound-proofed grids. But whimpers
seep through the mesh, the square holes—
partial thought piercing through tape
as thin as membrane. You reach the peak,
and stare above your knitted nation: green,
brown, blue, textile glue gunk; bruised
with flecks of seed beads that make you
sneeze. In the backyard, you dig and dig
and cough, pant and bury the consequences
of giving up on them. But sewing regret into
an heirloom, won't build you a gravestone.

spandex

you believe grey spandex
defeats the purpose
of spandex.
you say, *Malaka*,
it should be purple or pink.
fluorescent with a flash
of diagonal lime neon.
it should vibrate on skins
of 80s techno girls
with curls
and tats
from chewing gum packs.

yep, you're damn creative, I think.
i can tell you're a rapper (aspiring).

But doesn't grey spandex offer relief?

it's better at stretching
like rain clouds
over pubescent terrain,
above mountains
of flesh blooming
in adolescent
spring—hydrating.

under spandex
is sweat,
and grey averts
attention from the physics
of purposelessness

leaking
from teenage
swollen glands, (and yours)
and the birth of uncertainty;
the breath that fogs
the glass
when you make love
to the future
you've already lived.

You stare.

I wink and pass you the salt.

bandages

Take them off.
Show me your scars, seared
with the beauty of stunted decomposition—
Mother Earth's gift to seal pores and trap souls.
Let me touch Her bandages, Her preservation—
a shield against hurricanes and heat waves;
a weapon against air.
They are now your castle walls, your militia,
your peepholes—proof
of immortality.

Undress.

I want to see how you tear;
how She mummified
your intangible life.

what you found

Butter knife on edge of microwave
Chewed plastic cup in dishwasher
Drenched towel hanging over armchair
Butter knife in Motown CD stack
Greek coffee residue on foot stool
Dog shit next to toilet
Butter knife balanced on mesh lampshade
Sandy footprints on white-tiled wall
Faded brown bed sheet on clothes line
Butter knife on mouse pad
Marmalade flecks on fridge
Sticky fingerprints on remote
Butter knife by hairdryer
Butter knife in socket
Butter knife by my bath.

it was summer

the village street light
makes the gravel shine
like clusters
of black diamonds
where i buried
you alive.
you were dressed
in dirty linen
rather than
light orange cotton.
or perhaps
you'd have preferred
cheesecloth—cream—
to keep you cool
during Mediterranean
afternoons?
the sun makes my eyes bleed,
you'd say,
twisting your signet ring,
round, round,
off, on   *out, in*
you'd squash
your little knuckle
till it looked
like your frown

on the days
i'd go skinny
dipping
after you'd

touch me.

the gravel shines
like clusters
of black diamonds.
it was summer.

i wasn't afraid.

mustard

A wisp of fringe
bent a curled eyelash;
you blinked, sniffed
and flicked your head,
caramel curls brushing
against
the sleeve
of your mustard
mohair sweater.

The corner of your mouth
twitched—turned upward
in a well-intended smile.
You winked.
Your needles clicked.

But I saw scorn
and squinted at you,
sucking my tongue
to the roof
of my mouth,
thinking
you were trying
to outdo my knitting skills.

You were dying.

You didn't tell me.

dirty parsley
soils your frock;
hang the garlic chains

spicy toils
in battered tears
flavoured sorrow

fennel wilts between
hovering flies
to venus-trapezize

business files:
fraud steamed
in fish soup

raw butter snaps
add flavour
like crushed cloves

diluted sweat,
holy, curry spices
taste like misery

potato Mache
—the glue
for happy marriage

ONCE

Inspired by Echo and Narcissus

Love—it bounced on water. Once.
A skipping stone, though a cold
heart, it still made warmth

a woven shawl to soothe my longing.
Atoms trembled to make this devotion
a frantic sigh. But I have to say,

how could I not have known ardour was
moving, when our skin combined
because we were melting like ice in a warm lake?

***

Because we were melting like ice in a warm lake,
moving when our skin combined,
how could I not have known ardour was

a frantic sigh? But I have to say,
atoms trembled to make this devotion
a woven shawl to soothe my longing

heart. It still made warmth
a skipping stone. Though a cold
love, it bounced on water. Once.

goat skin beer holder

Panicked, but still
I sit watching you
in the local
kafeneion: dead
meat sipping
monotonous
juices
from cans
in leather gloves
that joke between themselves.

Crisps crackle
as you bite,
and swallow chunky
liquid yeast
like goat's blood and tripe.

You smack your lips
to the rhythms you chew
and sniff your snot
like leftovers.

Why don't you
just drink at home—
and save us the dough?

I know.

You can feel me watching.
And you want to flirt with blokes.

soap & silk

Our sweaty palms blend
like moist tongues—
they swing between
two shaking pairs
of legs; goat bells
jingle through thistly leaves,
introducing the speed
of a passing moped.

He looks left
He looks right
He looks up and down
the lampless street.
I grit my teeth
when his eyes focus
on the tip
of my nose
—*or is it my top lip?*

He grabs my breast
adorned in green
olive silk—he leans
towards me, camel breath—
tobacco ripe.
A pack of cigs
hits the ground
when our front teeth collide.

He vacuums my tongue
into a hole, I wish
I could wash
out with soap.
Bitter flushes
the rear of my throat.

I pull away, swallow,
wince, and vow
to never kiss
a 'God'
again.

not who i thought you were

What do I do
with the memories now?
How can I deem them
clean, like they were
before …
… this?

How do I know
your tickle frenzies
weren't filthy, guilty;
disfigured with thoughts
like …
… this?

What if your warmth,
so tender—my savior
from imperfect rage,
was simply a means to
see …
… this?

How do I look at you
now, in your gentle
plaid shirts, the man
I adored, when you have
become …
… this?

Can I really swallow
the disgust that erupts
like mushroom clouds
around my soul
after …
… this?

How dare they say
you are disabled,
sick, and offer
you support
for …
… this?

Are you still my father,
with soft almond eyes,
or a man who drank
thirty-five years
of …
… child porn?

city suicide

so tired … my eyes won't even cross—
stitch to form double vision blur.

your jagged voices poke
into my lungs, my head, injured
housing. domestic fights—spite
in fancy dress, cash,
tucked under my mattress …
no: floorboards; no …
tax man's brand new yacht.
my head … throbs.

digital spools of
… threaded,
comments … news reports,
keep knot—OUCH!—ing rational forms
of thought.

Don't touch me!

I pull the trigger, when I wake to you,
half-dressed in the cold crowd;
the government's
ineptitude
a razor to my wrist.

electric love

You hold my hand
as if holding heartache—careful
to not disturb
the eye of the riot
we need
to flee.

You stroke
my fingers—the five stages
of grief; massage
my knuckles with ease
and patience,
you'll never let go …

You make love
move like organza;
parallel energies
merging like cells
of Siamese twins.
No gas can blind love.

We are electric.

we Need women

Anthems bestow
copious discrimination;
egocentricity,
for glamorous history.
it just keeps lingering.
men never oppressed—
precious quests,
remorseless strength,
to utilize victory.
Without XX,
XY=Zero.

αυτοί

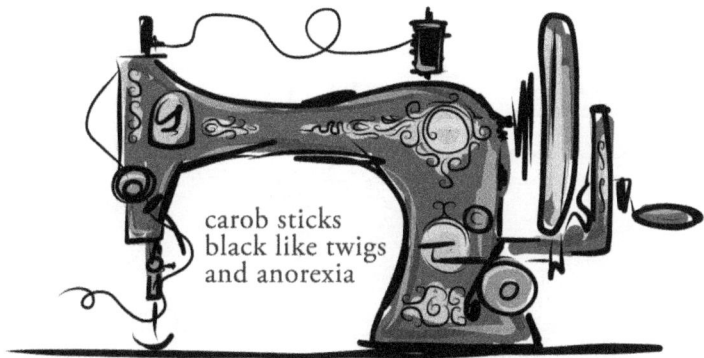

muscle of hammers
against steel—
winter buds

olive stains
obstruct the path
of neutral hope

red wine rims
round chipped lips
framed kiss

carob sticks
black like twigs
and anorexia

posh pink purse
in a chocolate box
—collection day

marmalade melodies
tune metallic tang:
soldered fillings

grey synthetic clouds
roosted in bruises
floating debt:

rag doll

She sits in *Yiayia's* treasure chest,
listening to footsteps
on floorboards.
She has holes in her face—
pin-pricks of children's dreams;
hollow freckles
filled with the last one hundred years.
But the deepest hole,
goes from her nostril,
through the back of her head,
made minutes before
a four-year-old girl
named Lila, died.
He had a swastika.
And a machine gun.

paper & ribbon

Carnival distorts moods, smiles, laughter,
must-eat food. Gossip hides the day's woes
with oral wrapping paper, bows.

But below lipstick stamps,
that paint pretty patterns
on our cheeks, are memories.

They augment as tears;
as years nibbled by wit that never warns.

loose yarn at midnight

misplaced moods
count moonshine
borders—rooted
among free | dom
and depend | ence

the sculpture

Museum hazard,
in magenta heels
hail!
for a cab
while soot-dusted men
pee
in rats' nests
peek
up skirts through drains.
Of course, it's Aphrodite, darling …
Rainwater rumbles,
umbrellas flick,
history remade
by stolen egos.

postpartum

"I just can't bear to lift my head
the world, it seems askew.
One more minute, here in bed,
then I swear I'll comfort you."

But baby wailed, hiccupped, cried,
and Mama did not move.
Instead she prayed her son might die,
knowing Papa would disapprove.

The baby's screams, grew louder still,
so Mama shook the crib.
"Shut up, I just don't have the will,
or I'll choke you with your bib."

She sunk her teeth into her skin,
wished pain to ease the hate.
The blood, it trickled down her chin,
and stained her with ill fate.

And then she sighed, thoughts in check,
hair wild, she gained strength,
she took her son by his neck,
and held him at arm's length.

She watched, as the baby's face
turned a cloudy blue,
when Papa came to offer grace;
restore his wife's virtue.

Papa fainted with a gasp,
the baby still midair.
But Mama did not free her grasp,
instead she stroked its hair.

the death of a queer athenian

the Athenian plucks,
ignorant to his open case
groomed with fountain gifts

his sterile breath is laced
with nicotine passion
—velvety twang—lining;
not only in his Mandolin's coffin.

his exhibitionist scars,
cuffed in black lingerie
are damage for ...

CRASH!

hammered, drunk minions
rotate ninety degrees
when the piano drops
from the balcony
flaunting granny knickers
murky muffles, muddy
puddles, *Lanterna* jingles ebb.

in city street jams,
Mamas shriek,
to the lingering chord of F.

the expatriate

Masking her twitching nose with chocolate
brown velvet gloves, Mrs. Cuthbert sneezes
indifference into faces of masked envy.

Brunettes squabble, rearrange the china—
mementos of when beauty became the new soul.

Balls of stilettoed feet, pitter patter round,
dressed in imaginary baby slips, over
floorboards polished with virgin sins.

Gilt façades lock minds reeking of burden,
faceted in diamond greed—reflections
distort impassive coat hangers, scented
closet doors, splintery, to infant fingers.

Foustanellas swindle gender bias—imperatives
pursed between penciled lips. Desire hides
in cotton jocks, inaccessible to Mrs. Cuthbert
who pretends to respect the cartridge belt
for another chance at being Greek.

Flapper-minded delights glint through her
glazed irises, as she threads the stare of knowledge
into every stitch, through her nip-tucked skin.

glossary

Section Headings: εγώ: me; εσύ: you; εμείς: us; αυτοί: them

mama's confession

Antoni mou: This means "my Antoni", which is in reference to the serial killer, Antonis Daglis (Greek: Αντώνης Δαγλής, born 1974), who was convicted of the murders of three women, and attempted murder of six others in Athens, Greece, on January 23, 1997. Also known as the "Athens Ripper", he was sentenced to thirteen terms of life imprisonment, plus 25 years.

breaking the curse

Euterpe (Greek: Ευτέρπη) was one of the Nine Muses, the muse of music, and lyric poetry. Her name was derived from the Ancient Greek ευ (well) + τέρπειν (to please), which as a whole means, "giver of much delight."

"gnidnib ym no gnitirw" is "writing on my binding" backwards. In ancient Greek magic, binding formulas were typically written on a type of voodoo doll, called a Kolossus, and writings were often written backwards to confuse the target. The binding of the doll represents tightly wrapping up a person or deity to prevent them

from moving.

monemvasia

Monemvasia (Greek: Μονεμβασία), meaning "single entrance", a Byzantine town initially constructed on a rock that was separated from the mainland during an earthquake in 375 AC, is located on a small peninsula off the east coast of the Peloponnese in Laconia, Greece. The fortress of Monemvasia dates back to the 6th Century. Since then it has changed hands several times. It was ruled by the Franks, Catalans, Ottomans, Byzantines and Venetians in succession.

sugar

Yiayia: Grandmother (Greek: Γιαγιά)

Papou: Grandfather (Greek: Παπού)

Halva: A traditional Greek sweet. (Greek: χαλβάς) Refers to the semolina-based version, rather than the sesame-based, which is made with one unit of oil, two of semolina, three of sugar and four of water.

spandex

Malaka: (Greek: μαλάκας) technically means "wanker", however, depending on the context, it is also used as "mate". It derives from the word *malakos* (μαλακός), which means "soft" or "spoilt".

what you found

Greek coffee residue: some people read their fortunes from the patterns the Greek coffee residue makes in their cups.

once

Echo and Narcissus: A Greek myth. In a nutshell, Echo was cursed so she would never be able to speak, but only say the last words of others. Narcissus was a man who fell in love with his own reflection. Echo fell in love with Narcissus, but she couldn't speak to him, only repeat his last words. She faded away from a broken heart. Narcissus, mesmerized by his own reflection never left the edge of the water. He too began to fade. And all that remained in his place was a flower, which took his name and, to this day, still lives by water.

not who i thought you were

6th stanza: In January, 2012, the Greek state announced that paedophiles were entitled to a 20-30% disability benefit.

rag doll

Yiayia: Grandmother (Greek: Γιαγιά). This poem was inspired by The Massacre of Kalavryta, when the extermination of the male population and the total destruction of this Greek town took place by German occupying forces during World War II, on 13 December 1943.

goat skin beer holder

kafeneion: (Greek: καφενείον) A traditional Greek coffee shop that also serves alcoholic beverages and *mezedes* (Greek: μεζέδες: a plate of mixed meats and cheeses, etc, to snack on). It is common for male village or town residents to congregate and socialize at their local coffee shop.

the death of a queer athenian

Lanterna: (Greek: Λαντέρνα) A human-sized music box with wheels. When the wheels turn, it plays music. They are often rolled through Athens' streets by elderly men to collect money.

the expatriate

Foustanella: (Greek: φουστανέλλα) a traditional skirt-like garment worn by men, similar to the kilt. A short *foustanella* is worn by ceremonial military units like the Presidential Guard.

Note from the author

When trying to look at the bigger picture we tend to forget the individual. We also tend to forget that it is the individual that contributes to the bigger picture. We, each and every one of us, uniquely influence the moral fabric of society. The "framework" of society is *us*, the choices we make, the actions we take, and the beliefs we embrace. They may be significant to some, and not so significant to others, but they nevertheless weave the fabric of our world together, creating perpetual causes and effects, both big and small. We contribute to one big massive cycle of life. And we are important. We matter.

With this in mind, I turned to numerology. You may have noticed that there are four parts, each consisting of seven poems. Each section begins with seven haiku (which do not conform to the rules due to my uncontrollable rebellion).

Why?

There are seven weekdays, seven levels of moral development, seven Archangels, and a seventh heaven. A rose with seven petals signifies seven directions of space, seven degrees of perfection, and seven planets (when it was thought there were only seven planets in the solar system). A rainbow has seven colours and, alchemically speaking, serves as a link to cross the gap between the ordinary and the enlightened.

Additionally, there are seven musical tones, which are connected to the colours of the rainbow. It is said that the employment of these notes and colours will provide a pathway to the evolution of consciousness.

In the Old Testament, seven appears 77 times, and symbolizes energy and moral principles. In the Egyptian religion, it symbolized eternal life, the whole cycle, a dynamic perfection. The phases of the moon each last for seven days, and after four phases, the lunar cycle is complete ($7 \times 4 = 28$). And the complete lunar cycle is the sum of the numbers in seven ($1 + 2 + 3 + 4 + 5 + 6 + 7 = 28$).

The sum of number four, the symbol of four sides of the Earth, and number three, the symbol of heaven, adds up to seven, which represents the universe in motion. Moreover, the three theological principles of goodness (faith, hope and mercy) plus the four cardinal principles of virtue (temperance, prudence, courage and justice) add up to seven: a symbol of a completely moral life.

All in all, seven symbolizes the stimulation of imagination and achieving results through conscious thought and awareness. Sure, this is all good and well in relation to the life cycle and the fabric of society, but how do the poems in this collection entirely relate to a number which ultimately deals with perfection, when the characters depicted within are full of flaws? Let me repeat Doug Coupland's quote from the beginning of the book: *When we constantly ask for miracles, we're unraveling the fabric of the world. A world of continuous miracles would not be a world, it would be a cartoon.*

To me, seven represents symmetry, reason, and order within the universe. Even when life seems chaotic, there is an omnipresent fabric that is reassuringly homogeneous in its behaviour. We are all imperfect humans. We will be what we will be. And we are perfect just the way we are.

acknowledgements

Many thanks to the editors of the following literary journals and anthologies who published a few of the poems from this collection: *Mediterranean Poetry, Women's Work, Mirror Dance, Apeiron Review, Short, Fast & Deadly, Eunoia Eeview, Hermeneutic Chaos, Poetry Repairs*, and to ABC Radio Australia for reciting the poem *Sugar* on their *Poetica* program.

A very special thanks to my magnificent parents, Erika Bach and Demetri Vlass, for being here for me no matter what I choose to do, and for gifting me with the gene of creativity; to my partner, Spilios Tzemos, for his undying support and help with Greek trivia; to Dawn Ius for her valuable instincts and perpetual availability to boost my ego; and to Angela Felsted for her poetry critiques, expert opinions, and prompt replies to my desperate advice-seeking emails while working on this collection.

And of course, a very special thanks to Amie McCracken for her enormous help in producing *The Bell Collection* edition.

Enjoyed this book?
Go to *vineleavespress.com/books*
to find more from *The Bell Collection.*

To sign up to Jessica's newsletter
and/or connect with her on social media
go to *jessicabellauthor.com/contact.*

Are you a writer?
You might be interested in Jessica's
Writing in a Nutshell series.

www.ingramcontent.com/pod-product-compliance
Lightning Source LLC
Chambersburg PA
CBHW051737040426
42447CB00008B/1184